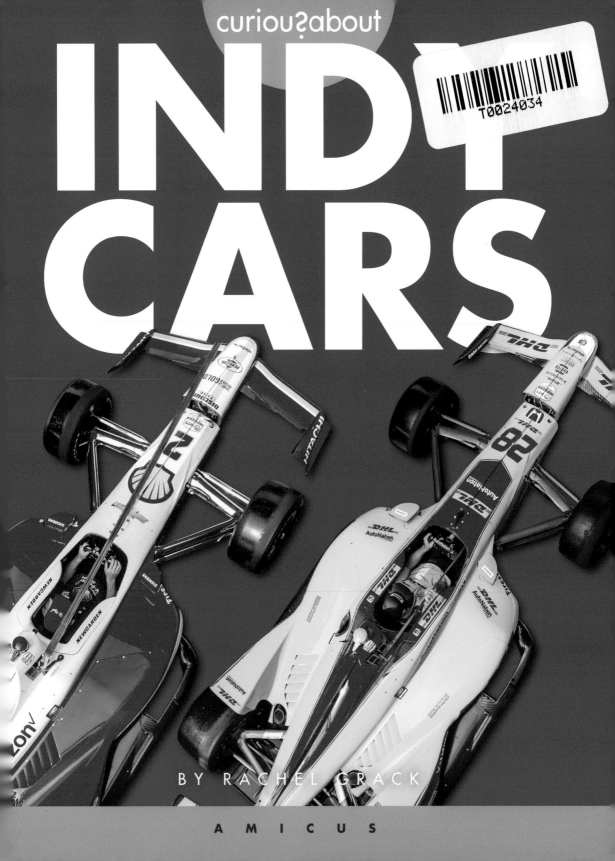

curiou♀about
INDY CARS

BY RACHEL GRACK

T0024034

AMICUS

What are you

curious about?

Curious About is published by
Amicus
P.O. Box 227
Mankato, MN 56002
www.amicuspublishing.us

Copyright © 2023 Amicus.
International copyright reserved in all countries.
No part of this book may be reproduced in any
form without written permission from the publisher.

Editors: Gillia Olson and Alissa Thielges
Designer: Kathleen Petelinsek
Photo researcher: Bridget Prehn

Library of Congress Cataloging-in-Publication Data
Names: Koestler-Grack, Rachel A., 1973- author.
Title: Curious about Indy cars / by Rachel Grack.
Description: Mankato, Minnesota : Amicus, [2023] | Series:
Curious about cool rides | Includes bibliographical references
and index. | Audience: Ages 6–9. | Audience: Grades 2–3.
Identifiers: LCCN 2020001127 (print) | LCCN 2020001128
(ebook) | ISBN 9781645491163 (library binding) | ISBN
9781681526836 (paperback) | ISBN 9781645491583 (pdf)
Subjects: LCSH: Indy cars—Juvenile literature. |
Automobile racing—Juvenile literature.
Classification: LCC TL236.25 .K64 2023 (print) | LCC
TL236.25 (ebook) | DDC 629.228/5—dc23
LC record available at https://lccn.loc.gov/2020001127
LC ebook record available at https://lccn.loc.gov/2020001128

Photos © Shutterstock/Grindstone Media Group cover, 1, 3, 12,
19 (helmet, head sock); Shutterstock/Jon Nicholls Photography
4–5; Alamy/imageBROKER 6–7 (Indy); Shutterstock/Stuart Elflett
6–7 (F1); Shutterstock/Sergei Bachlakov 8–9; 20–21;iStock/
schlol 10; AP/Jeff McIntosh 2, 11; Shutterstock/Vector
Tradition 13 (tickets); iStock/kvsan 13 (engine); Shutterstock/
risteski goce 13 (tire); iStock/Pixelci 13 (chassis); Shutterstock/
Lotus_studio 13 (wrench); Library of Congress/Carol M.
Highsmith 14–15; Alamy/Cal Sport Media 16-17; Shutterstock/
HodagMedia 19 (top); Shutterstock/GARAGE38 19 (gloves)

What are Indy cars?

They are race cars. Indy cars have open wheels and open **cockpits**. They are named after the Indianapolis (Indy) 500. Indy cars reach speeds of 230 miles per hour (370 kph). They go from 0 to 60 miles per hour (97 kph) in 3 seconds!

Zoom! Hélio Castroneves raced in the 2017 Honda Indy.

Indy Car

How are Indy cars different from other race cars?

Formula
One Car

Indy cars look a lot like Formula One race cars. But Formula One cars race worldwide. Indy cars race mainly in North America. NASCAR uses stock race cars. They look more like regular cars. They have closed wheels and cockpits.

INDY CAR	VS.	FORMULA ONE
2.2-liter V-6 engine		1.6-liter V-6 engine
no electric assist		electric assist
no power steering		power steering
0 to 60 in 3 seconds		0 to 60 in 2.1 seconds
top speed:		top speed:
235 mph (378 kph)		200 mph (322 kph)

What kind of fuel do Indy cars use?

A car makes a pit stop in the Molson Indy.

It's called E85-R. This fuel is 85 parts **ethanol** and 15 parts gas. The mix gives engines more power. It burns cleaner than gas alone. It also gets more miles per gallon. That means fewer **pit stops** to fill up.

What kind of tires do Indy cars use?

Big tires called slicks. Slicks are smooth with no treads. They grip the track. Indy cars go through 360 tires a season. Why so many? Racing speeds cause **downforce**. Cars become four times heavier. That weight is hard on tires!

Slick tires wear down fast during races.

How much does an Indy car cost?

A lot of time and money go into each Indy car.

Indy cars cost at least $1 million. Cars sometimes go through two engines for one race. Plus, teams pay drivers and **pit crews**. They buy tools and tires. One season could add up to $15 million!

$21,000

INDY 500 ENTRANCE FEE: $21,000

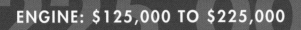

$225,000

ENGINE: $125,000 TO $225,000

$91,000

TIRES: $91,000 (ONE MONTH SUPPLY)

$350,000

CHASSIS (CAR FRAME): $350,000

$250,000

MECHANICS / STAFF: $250,000

Where do Indy cars race?

Indy cars race on three kinds of tracks. Oval tracks are also called **speedways**. They are closed tracks used only for racing. Street circuits are set up on public roads. Road courses look like public roads but are used for racing only.

DID YOU KNOW?
A superspeedway is at least 2 miles (3.2 km) long.

The Indy 500 oval track is 2.5 miles (4.0 km) long.

What's a race like?

Drivers line up
at the start of
Indy 500.

First, cars run laps to **qualify**. Finish times set the starting order. For the race, cars line up in rows. A green flag drops, and the race begins. The Indy 500 is 200 laps. It takes about 3 hours to finish.

How does it feel behind the wheel?

Driving is a hard workout! Braking is hard on legs and feet. It's like pushing a 100-pound (45-kg) weight. Racers brake about every 18 seconds! Steering feels like twisting a heavy truck tire. They do that for a few hours straight. Whew!

Drivers stay in tip-top shape to compete.

Kevlar helmet

Fire-resistant head sock and one-piece firesuit

DID YOU KNOW?
The driver wears gear to protect them if the car catches fire.

Fire-resistant gloves

What happens during a pit stop?

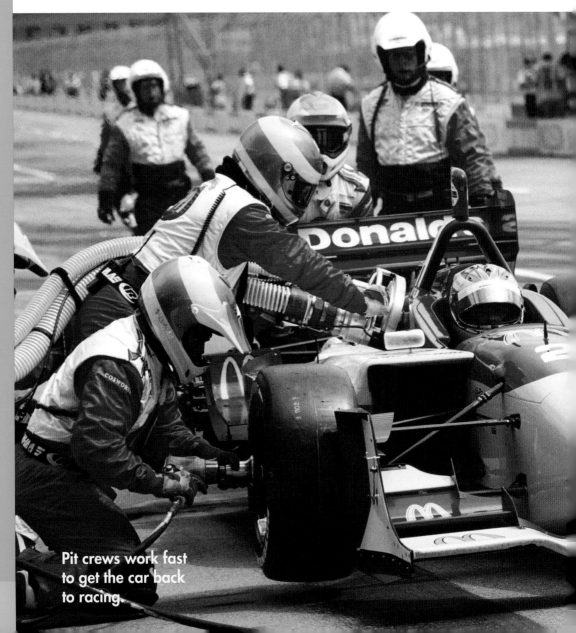

Pit crews work fast to get the car back to racing.

Pit crews add fuel and change the tires. They do it in about eight seconds! It takes great teamwork and no mistakes. Every second counts in Indy car races. Vroom!

DID YOU KNOW?
The average pit stop is 8 seconds. All four tires can be changed in 5 seconds!

ASK MORE QUESTIONS

What's it like at an Indy car racetrack?

How close are the races?

Try a BIG QUESTION: What dangers do Indy car drivers face?

SEARCH FOR ANSWERS

Search the library catalog or the Internet.
A librarian, teacher, or parent can help you.

Using Keywords
Find the looking glass.

Keywords are the most important words in your question.

?

If you want to know about

- Indy car race events, type: INDY CAR RACES

- Indy car races with close finishes type: INDY CAR CLOSE RACES

FIND GOOD SOURCES

Here are some good, safe sources you can use in your research.
Your librarian can help you find more.

Books

Cool Indy Cars by Jon M. Fishman, 2019.

Indy Cars by Marysa Storm, 2020.

Internet Sites

NTT IndyCar Series: Race Videos
https://www.indycar.com/Videos
This is the official site for Indy car racing news. Be aware of ads on the site that try to sell you things.

Top Gear: Closest Finishes in the History of Motor Racing
https://www.topgear.com/car-news/ gallery-closest-finishes-history-motor-racing#1
Top Gear is a show on the BBC. The BBC is a respected source of news and other programming.

Every effort has been made to ensure that these websites are appropriate for children. However, because of the nature of the Internet, it is impossible to guarantee that these sites will remain active indefinitely or that their contents will not be altered.

SHARE AND TAKE ACTION

Go racing!
Find a go-kart racing park near you. Ask your parents to take you on a race-day field trip.

Hold a pinewood derby car race with your friends.
Make a dragstrip on your front sidewalk. Take turns, and see who wins.

Build an Indy car model.
Buy an Indy car model kit from a local hobby store. Ask an adult to help you put it together.

GLOSSARY

cockpit The place where drivers sit; Indy cars have open cockpits.

downforce A force that acts on a moving car, pushing it down toward the ground.

ethanol Fuel made with an alcohol from plants.

pit crew The members of a racing team who repair the car.

pit stop A short stop during a race to service cars.

qualify To be able to participate in an event.

speedway An oval racetrack; a superspeedway is at least 2 miles (3.2 km) long.

INDEX

About the Author

Rachel Grack has been editing and writing children's books since 1999. She lives on a ranch in Arizona. Hot cars have always fired her up! At one time, she even owned a street rod—a 1965 Ford Galaxie 500. She loved cruising with the windows down. This series refueled her passion for cool rides!